Welcome to Avery's Garden

Angel Inspired heARTwork for Bereaved Families

This book is dedicated to my son, Avery R. Denz, forever my angel, forever my muse. He was born still on June 17, 2016. My husband and I said goodbye to our son at 20 weeks and 4 days gestation as I was diagnosed with an incompetent cervix. As I searched for meaning in life after loss, I found comfort in other angel mothers who, like myself, were searching for ways to remember their children.

As I continued on my journey, I came to realize how important it was to preserve Avery's memory and to give back to a community that welcomed me so kindheartedly.

I began using my artistic gifts to honor babies that had grown their wings as they left this Earth. This outlet for my grief has been used in several projects and most recently in Avery's Garden- Grief Journal. This is when the idea for the coloring book came to light.

The drawings included in this book were inspired in loving memory of Avery and other precious babies gone too soon. Each bereaved mother who participated, came forward with angel names, signs and symbols and special quotes or phrases that were unique to their memory. Each drawing was done by hand with love, kindness and understanding to those effected by infant loss.

As you color each drawing, please take a moment to reflect on the dedication pages for each angel. May these pages give light to your grief and peace to your heart.

Avery's Garden

In loving memory of Avery

In Avery's Garden, you will find the magic of beautiful blooming flowers and the wonder of small creatures such as bees and butterflies. The flowers in this drawing represent flowers planted in the first outdoor garden to honor Avery in June of 2016.

In the Summer of 2016, as I mourned in grief, I would visit his garden. I would watch as nature provided beauty to his special space. The roses would burst with bright pinks and reds while the whimsical celosia flowers stood tall. I would sit and admire all the life that bloomed and buzzed in the sweet sunlight.

Each year I will continue to plant a garden in honor of my baby.

Tree of Bravery

In loving memory of Thorin

The Tree of Bravery represents Thorin and the 142 days he spent on this Earth. There are 141 leaves on the tree and 1 falling leaf that is special for the daring angel. The Tree of Bravery has strong roots and beauty that can be seen for miles.

Garden Birds

In loving memory of Jensen

Jensen's angel often visits in the form of a bird. This special sign to his family is a reminder when he is near. It is often said that a bird is a messenger serving as a sign for those who are looking.

<u>Gavin's Garden</u>

In loving memory of Gavin

Gavin sends his mommy signs of hearts and beautiful green butterflies. His memory is rejoiced in the thoughts of a garden where his mommy can whisper sweet messages of love.

Dream Catcher

In loving memory of Everlee

Everlee is one of Avery's very close friends. They share moments together to help guide their families to love and hope. The dream catcher featured is a representation of friendship, love and light that is captured. The bad dreams flow down the special woven fabrics and release away from all the good surrounding the angels. The leaf represents a sunset dedication project Everlee was included in during October 2016.

Forever
-Everlee Lasting Friends-

<u>Everlee's Garden</u>

In loving memory of Everlee

Welcome to Everlee's Garden. As you enter through the old doors and twinkling gates, you will find the path towards love and remembrance. The garden often captures both beautiful sunrises and the evening setting sun. Everlee's garden is a place to go for tranquility.

This drawing is a recreation of the garden her family created in her honor. Everlee's symbol forever will be a sunflower.

A sunflower is a symbol of adoration, loyalty and longevity.

<u>Forever in my Heart</u>

In loving memory of Avery

Avery often sends signs in the form of iridescent rain clouds. In the sky you will find a hidden rainbow giving off beautiful colors. The angel chime is representation of a gift given after Avery's passing. It has become a symbol of love and remembrance for my angel.

The bee on the flower is special to the deep love of photography that flourished after Avery's passing. Finding beauty in even the smallest details in nature has brought light within the grief. The leaves are special to the sunset dedication done for Avery on October 31, 2016, which would have been his due date.

"In the morning when I wake, and the sun is coming through, oh you fill my lungs with sweetness, and you fill my head with you."
(Bloom-The Paper Kites).

Cardinals in the Garden

In loving memory of Avery

After Avery passed away, a cardinal appeared. This cardinal visited every day and still does even today. The cardinal bird sings from the roof tops and the trees. He has become a symbol for Avery.

In his garden there is a rose tree planted and many different flowers. The beauty of this memorial space bursts with colors and brings peace to a hurting heart.

Allowing your hands to meet with the Earth in the form of a memorial garden provides a space for reflection, beauty and growth for the soul.

"Can I take it to the morning
Where the fields are
painted gold
And the trees are filled
with memories
Of the feelings never told?

When the evening pulls
the sun down,
And the day is almost through,
Oh, the whole world is sleeping,
But my world is you."
(Bloom-The Paper Kites).

Holly Sprigs and Berries

In loving memory of Holly

Holly's symbol is a beautiful red a green sprig of holly with berries. Her mommy imagines that she would have loved nature and being in the woods. The special quote can be found where she rests peacefully.

Holly represents eternal life. Some ancient traditions would also hang it as it is known to bring luck and protection.

Sugar Skull in the Garden

In loving memory of Lucas

The meaning of a sugar skull is when you wish to remember someone special. The sugar skull for Lucas is in remembrance of his precious life. The roses that surround the ornate sugar skull represent a union of Lucas forever in Avery's Garden.

Lucas is the baby of a close personal friend. She graciously took care of the arrangements for Avery and shared the story of her son as I mourned. As we joined arms as angel mothers, I found comfort in the passage written next to the sugar skull that is on Avery's mass card.

<u>The Tree of Hearts</u>

In loving memory of Cullin

This is the tree of hearts and symbolizes sweet baby Cullin. His mommy finds hearts in so many beautiful ways. Cullin's hearts are found in the sky and on the grounds of the Earth. In this drawing, there are many hearts. Some are easy to spot, while others require you to look a little closer. These hearts not only represent love, but the hope that there is beauty to be found in the journey in life after loss.

Pennies Amongst the Flowers

In loving memory of Harvi

Harvi is remembered by her family as being their sweet little miss, and their very own angel. She brings them butterflies and leaves pennies along the way.

In this special drawing for Harvi you will find pennies. Some are easily spotted, while others may test your imagination. The butterflies can be found dancing between the flowers that bloom for her beautiful remembrance.

Kian's Clock

In loving memory of Kian

It is said that we often don't remember days, we remember moments.

This clock was drawn in memory of Kian. He was born at 10:00 p.m. Time seems to slow down and then speed up in a garden. The Earth slowly releases a bloom which grows into a magnificent flower. Although a flower may wilt or even die, the promise that a new one will form is one of creations greatest gifts.

Allowing yourself the time to grieve is one of the kindest gifts you can give to your heart.

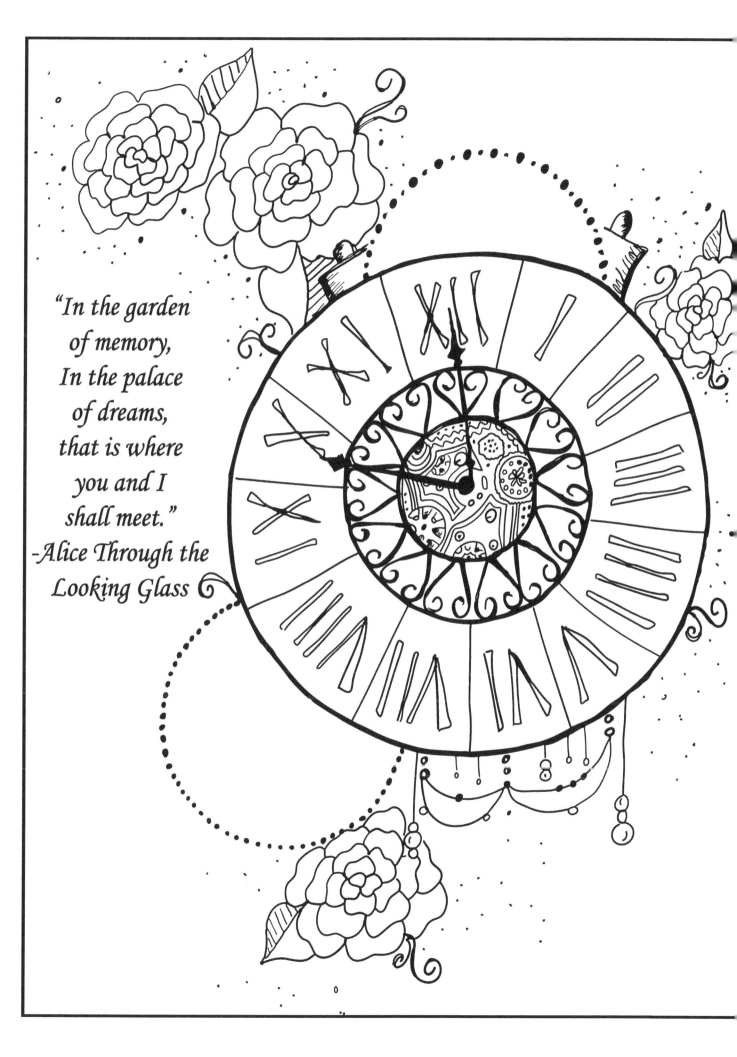

<u>Capture Your Grief</u>

In loving memory of Christian

Welcome to Christian's beach memorial.

In the center of the page is a flower mandala. The mandala appears to us in all aspects of life, the Earth, the Sun, the Moon and the circles of life encompassing friends, family and communities.

Christian recently had his 10th angelversary. His mommy is a beautiful soul that offers support to grieving hearts.

Christian's Beach

In loving memory of Christian

The seashore of remembrance has become an important part of Christian's mommy's journey. Flowers are arranged on the sand of the beach, where artwork is created. As the waves roll in and the sun sets, the love is release through these images.

"Raise my hands, paint my spirit gold. Bow my head, Keep my heart slow And I will wait, I will wait for you."
—Mumford & Sons

Christian

Flowers in Heaven's Garden

In loving memory of Janelle

Janelle is represented in this drawing by wilting flowers that show that she was picked and taken away too soon.

"Just as dew refreshes the wilted flower, tenderness restores a grieving heart."- Unknown

<u>Primrose Iris Garden</u>

In loving memory of Primrose

Welcome to Primrose Iris Garden. Her parents planted a memorial garden for her with an arrangement of beautiful flowers. This garden is a place of honor, beauty and love.

Maybel's Magnolia

In loving memory of Maybel

Maybel's mommy is a dear friend of mine. She was able to spend 99 days with her baby before she grew her wings. The magnolia tree represents a gift she gave me when Avery passed away. There are 99 leaves on the tree to represent each beautiful day she spent on this Earth. The double rainbow in the background are for my friend's two Earth children. Maybel had her 12th angelversary on the day this entry was done.

<u>Heaven's Sandbox</u>

In loving memory of Maria Paz

Maria is a world away, but never forgotten. Her mommy sang her songs as she spent time in the hospital. She is remembered with delicate ballerinas on the outfit she wore when she grew her wings.

This entry is a celebration of the short life she had on this Earth.

She soars on angel wings, flies with butterflies and plays in Heaven's sandbox.

"Watch all the flowers...

Dance with the wind...

Listen to snowflakes...

Whisper your name."

(Fly to Your Heart, Selena Gomez)

<u>Cherry Blossoms</u>

In loving memory of Natalie

Natalie is remembered with beautiful cherry blossoms.
In some cultures, the cherry blossom represents the fragility and the beauty of life.

Rose and Her Lily

In loving memory of Lily

This drawing is a moon made up of lily flowers. They bloom in the sky for her. The roses light up as the butterflies dance in Lily's memory.

Moses Garden

In loving memory of Moses

Welcome to Moses Garden. Here all the beautiful flowers and thistles bloom in his honor. In some cultures it is said that a thistle is a representation of bravery, devotion, durability, strength and determination.

Come Fly With Me

In loving memory of Leona Grace

Leona is remembered with peonies and sends hearts and hummingbirds to her family.

She sent the first hummingbird while her family listened to music from Frank Sinatra.

<u>Aloha Angels</u>

In loving memory of Pualani Iris and Ku'uMaka Poppy

Pualani and Ku'uMaka are twins with family ties to Hawaii. Classic Pooh Bear cubbies represent these sweet angels. Both angels have a flower as a middle name which only adds to the magnificent wonders of Heaven's Garden.

Ku'umaka means "The apple of my eye"
Pualani means "Heavenly Flower"

Avery's Garden

Email: averysgarden16@gmail.com

To follow me on social media please visit the sites below. If you would like to make a donation toward my ongoing project for Avery's Garden Treehouse Retreat, please visit:
https://www.gofundme.com/averys-garden-treehouse-retreat

 Instagram: @averysgarden

 Facebook: Avery's Garden

Thank you for your purchase and support for the bereaved families of infant loss. Creating art for the angel babies and their families has been an honor.

#averysgardengriefjournal

Made in the USA
Middletown, DE
22 July 2019